CONTENTS

Words appearing in the text in bold, **like this**, are explained in the glossary.

Look out for these boxes:

WHAT WOULD YOU DO?
Imagine what it would be like to make difficult choices in wartime.

REMEMBERING BRAVERY
Find out about the ways in which we remember courageous acts today.

NUMBER CRUNCHING
Learn the facts and figures about wars and battles.

SECRET HEROES
Find out about the brave individuals who didn't make it into the history books.

INTRODUCTION

Timbers split, spears fly, and men shout battle cries. Driven along by two sails and 170 rowers, Greek **triremes** cut through the waves at 13 kilometres (8 miles) per hour. The Greeks row straight at their Persian enemies. Their **rams** smash into the wooden Persian ships. The Greeks hurl arrows, spears, and burning oil. The Persian ships burn and sink.

UNKNOWN HEROES

Most of the sailors at the battle of Salamis are unknown heroes today. Historians think that Eurybiades of Sparta, a city in ancient Greece, led the Greek sailors.

Brian Williams

Raintree

www.raintreepublishers.co.uk
Visit our website to find out more information about Raintree books.

To order:

☎ Phone 0845 6044371

🖨 Fax +44 (0) 1865 312263

✉ Email myorders@raintreepublishers.co.uk

Customers from outside the UK please telephone +44 1865 312262

Raintree is an imprint of Capstone Global Library Limited, a company incorporated in England and Wales having its registered office at 7 Pilgrim Street, London, EC4V 6LB – Registered company number: 6695582

Edited by Louise Galpine and Vaarunika Dharmapala
Designed by Clare Webber and Steve Mead
Original illustrations © Capstone Global Library Ltd 2011
Illustrated by KJA-Artists.com
Picture research by Elizabeth Alexander
Originated by Capstone Global Library Ltd
Printed and bound in China by Leo Paper Products Ltd

ISBN 978 1 406 22199 2 (hardback)
15 14 13 12 11
10 9 8 7 6 5 4 3 2 1

ISBN 978 1 406 22207 4 (paperback)
16 15 14 13 12
10 9 8 7 6 5 4 3 2 1

British Library Cataloguing in Publication Data
Williams, Brian.
Sailors under fire. – (War stories)
359'.009-dc22
A full catalogue record for this book is available from the British Library.

Acknowledgements
We would like to thank the following for permission to reproduce photographs: Alamy pp. **6** (© North Wind Picture Archives), **8** (© Pictorial Press Ltd), **12** (© North Wind Picture Archives), **16** (© INTERFOTO); Corbis pp. **4** (© Bettmann), **10** (© Fine Art Photographic Library), **18** (© Schenectady Museum; Hall of Electrical History Foundation), **21** (Bettmann), **24** (© Reuters), **26** (© Carlos Dias/epa); Getty Images pp. **5** (Popperfoto), **7** (Stock Montage), **17** (Hulton Archive), **23** (Topical Press Agency); Photolibrary p. **19** (Douglas Peebles); Public domain p. **15**; Shutterstock background design and features (© oriontrail), p. **11** (© stocker1970).

Cover photograph of Pearl Harbor reproduced with permission of the Kobal Collection (Touchstone/Jerry Bruckheimer INC).

We would like to thank John Allen Williams for his invaluable help in the preparation of this book.

Every effort has been made to contact copyright holders of material reproduced in this book. Any omissions will be rectified in subsequent printings if notice is given to the publisher.

Battles at sea

This happened in 480 BC, at the battle of Salamis. It was the first famous sea battle in history. Before this, battles had been fought on land.

Ever since Salamis, sailors have been facing their enemies in war. Both the ships and the weapons of war they carry have been getting more powerful and deadly.

By the AD 1600s, warships carried guns. In the 1800s, iron **battleships** used the power of steam to travel faster. Today, we have **aircraft carriers**, **destroyers**, and **submarines** that use technologies undreamt of in the time of the ancient Greeks and Persians.

The courage of sailors

War stories tell us about the courage of men and women at sea. Every sailor, from the captain to the cook, has a job to do.

In battle, it is normal for sailors to get scared. Their training helps them to do their duty: to obey orders, and to keep their ship fighting and afloat.

Sea battles sometimes end with ships sinking, and sailors must swim for their lives. A cold sea can kill a person in minutes, and hungry sharks may gather.

Sailors may spend many days in lifeboats waiting for rescue. All these dangers mean that sailors often help each other out. They help friends, and often enemies, too. After all, they all face the same danger: the sea.

▲ These sailors are waiting to be rescued after a World War II battle which sank their ship. Hanging on to the barrel helps them stay afloat.

◄ At Salamis, the Greek ships rammed into the Persians.

5

SAILING-SHIP BATTLES

Sailing-ship battles were slow between the 400s BC and the AD 1800s. Sailing ships can go only where the wind blows them, so two **fleets** might take hours or days to get close enough to fire their **cannons**.

The Armada fire-ships

Wooden ships burned easily. In 1588, Spain's mighty **Armada** attacked England. During days of sea-battle, the English sent blazing fire-ships in among the Spanish ships. The Spanish sailors called them "Hell-burners". The Armada escaped, but was blown away by a great storm. Only 61 out of 130 ships got home, and 15,000 brave men drowned.

▲ This painting shows English and Spanish ships during the Armada battles of 1588.

Who was John Paul Jones?

John Paul Jones was born in Scotland in 1747 and went to America when he was 12. At that time, Britain ruled 13 American colonies. In 1776, the colonies launched the Revolutionary War against the British. They won their independence and became the United States. Jones became a hero because he was a commander in the US Navy which helped win the war.

▶ John Paul Jones first went to sea aged 12, and was a captain at 22.

Dangerous work

The ships Jones sailed had two or three tall wooden masts with twenty or more canvas sails. Rows of cannon lined the decks. A sailor's life was hard and dangerous. Boys went to sea as young as 12. They had to climb the masts to fix the sails, even in a storm. Some sailors fell to their deaths. Others were washed over the side in rough seas. Many were drowned in shipwrecks.

Bonhomme Richard

Jones liked a fast ship. He thought the ship he had been given to fight the British, *Bonhomme Richard*, was too old and slow, so he rebuilt it. "I intend to go in harm's way," he said, meaning he would attack, whatever the danger.

▼ This painting shows *Bonhomme Richard* (centre) battling the British in 1779.

Why was a fast ship best?

A fast ship could get into position first to fire its cannon. Cannon balls could rip sails, break masts, make holes in oak planks, knock off a sailor's head or leg, or send wood splinters flying, causing terrible injuries.

The battle with the *Serapis*

In 1779, Jones fought the British ships *Serapis*, which had 50 guns, and *Countess of Scarborough*, which had 22 guns. The fight began badly for Jones.

One of *Bonhomme Richard*'s guns blew up and the ship began to sink. The British captain asked the Americans to surrender. Upon hearing this, Jones is said to have shouted, "I have not yet begun to fight!"

In the end, it was the British who had to give up. Jones and his sailors jumped on to *Serapis* as their own ship went down. They had captured two British ships, and Jones became a hero.

REMEMBERING BRAVERY

John Paul Jones died in 1792 and was buried at the United States Naval Academy in Annapolis, Maryland. His bravery and daring still inspire the young men and women who train there. The words on his tomb read, "He gave to our navy its earliest traditions of heroism and victory."

Admiral Nelson

Jones never fought Horatio Nelson, who was an English naval hero. Nelson was born in Norfolk in 1758. Like Jones, he went to sea at the age of 12. Nelson suffered many injuries in battle. In 1794, he lost his sight in one eye. In 1797, a doctor had to cut off his right arm after he was shot. Despite his wounds, Nelson became an admiral.

WHAT WOULD YOU DO?

Powder-monkeys were small boys who carried **gunpowder** to the guns. It was dangerous work, with cannon balls flying and sailors getting killed. Could you have done your duty? Would it have been better to hide, or even jump overboard?

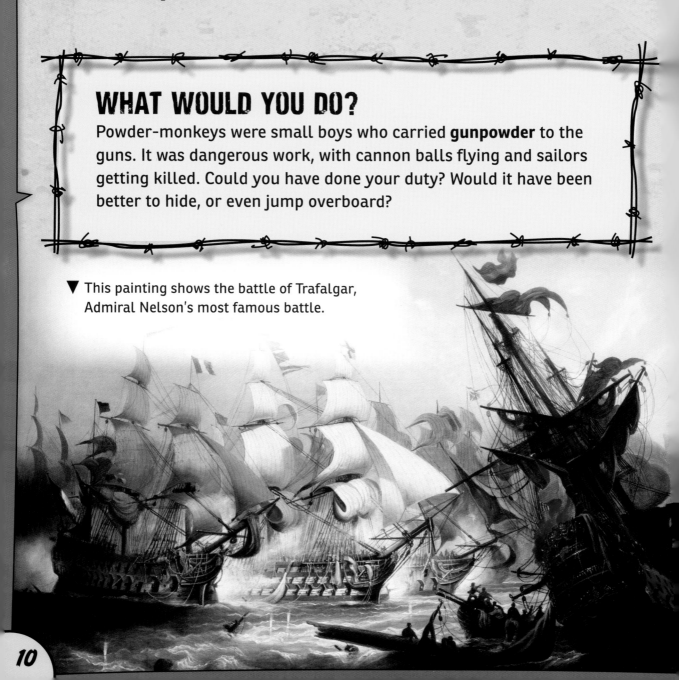

▼ This painting shows the battle of Trafalgar, Admiral Nelson's most famous battle.

Broadsides and deck-fights

Nelson's most famous battle was in 1805 at Cape Trafalgar, off the coast of Spain. Led by his own ship *Victory*, his fleet of 27 beat 33 French and Spanish ships. The biggest ships had 100 guns. When they were far apart, they fired broadsides (when every gun along one side fired in turn) at each other. When the ships were close together, sailors fought with swords and pistols on deck.

During the battle, a French sailor sitting high up on a mast aimed and shot at Nelson, who was below on deck. Nelson died three hours later, but he knew the battle had been won. "Thank God I have done my duty," he said.

▶ Admiral Nelson's ship *Victory* survives to this day and is docked at Portsmouth.

REMEMBERING BRAVERY

Admiral Nelson was buried in St Paul's Cathedral, London. People can honour his memory every time they look up at his statue on top of Nelson's Column in Trafalgar Square in London.

THE AGE OF IRONCLAD BATTLESHIPS

By the mid 1800s, steamships were replacing wooden sailing ships. These new ships were known as ironclads because they were covered with iron armour for protection.

The Battle of Mobile Bay

In 1864, during the American **Civil War** between the **Union** and the **Confederates**, ironclads met in battle. Union Admiral David G. Farragut led 18 ships into Mobile Bay, Alabama. Four were ironclads and the rest were wooden ships. Confederate Admiral Franklin Buchanan had only one ironclad, named *Tennessee*.

Cannon balls simply bounced off *Tennessee*. But one of Farragut's ironclads, *Tecumseh*, was hit by a **mine** and sank. Even iron was no defence against this underwater weapon. The battle did not end until *Tennessee* could no longer move or shoot, and the captain was forced to surrender.

REMEMBERING BRAVERY

As *Tecumseh* was sinking, the crew abandoned ship. Captain Tunis Craven paused at the steps to the deck, to let his crewmate Pilot John Collins go up first. Collins escaped but Captain Craven drowned, along with 92 sailors. *Tecumseh* still lies at the bottom of Mobile Bay. The United States Coast Guard protects the wreck, in honour of the men who died.

◄ Here you can see how Union and Confederate ships met in battle at Mobile Bay.

◄ The ironclad *Tennessee* was attacked on all sides by Union ships.

What lesson did this battle teach?

Mobile Bay showed that even though ironclads had been thought to be unsinkable, they could successfully be attacked from underwater. By 1900, ironclad **battleships** had bigger guns and even thicker armour. Once again, these ships were thought to be unsinkable. And once again, another battle showed that this was not true.

The battle fleet that sailed around the world

In 1904, Russia and Japan were at war. A **fleet** of Russian ironclads steamed around the world to reach Japan. From Russia, they sailed around Europe, south around Africa, and east to Singapore. Then, the battle fleet headed for Japan.

Why was it such an adventure?

The voyage took seven months. For officer-cadet Wernher von Kursel, this was an amazing adventure. He came from Latvia, then part of Russia. He had never been so far from home. He was proud of his ship, the battleship *Suvorov*.

Some of von Kursel's shipmates had never been on a ship before. Life at sea seemed strange to them. One of the dirtiest jobs was that of a stoker, who had to shovel coal to burn in the ship's steam engines. It was a relief for the sailors to step ashore on sunny islands in the Indian Ocean or in South East Asia. Sailors would come back to the ships with monkeys, parrots, and straw hats!

NUMBER CRUNCHING

Suvorov was launched in 1902. It was 121 metres (400 feet) in length and weighed 14,000 tonnes. Its top speed was about 16 **knots**, or 30 kilometres (19 miles) per hour. It had 56 guns.

Pride of the fleet

Von Kursel's ship was the **flagship** of the fleet. In command of the ship was Captain Ignatzius. He made everyone work hard because the fleet's commander Admiral Rozhestvensky was on board, too. Not all Russian ships were in good shape like the *Suvorov*. Some broke down, and many of the sailors had not been trained to fire the guns.

▼ The battleship *Suvorov* was the pride of the Russian Navy.

The Battle of Tsushima

On 27 May 1905, the Japanese fleet commander Admiral Togo and his sailors saw black coal-smoke on the horizon. The Russians were steaming into battle. The fleets fought in Tsushima Strait, between Japan and Korea. For Wernher von Kursel, it was to be his first and last battle.

▲ This illustration shows the battle of Tsushima.

Opening fire

The Japanese fired from 6 kilometres (3.5 miles) away. Their shells smashed the Russian ships into burning wrecks. Yet the Russians kept firing back. Captain Ignatzius was wounded, but kept *Suvorov* fighting. With his head bandaged, he shouted, "We must put out the fires. Follow me!" As he ran to fight the flames, a Japanese shell exploded near him. The captain was killed instantly.

The *Suvorov* sinks

Admiral Rozhestvensky was knocked out and taken to another ship. One by one, *Suvorov*'s guns fell silent. A Russian ship tried to rescue the crew, but there was not enough room for everyone. Von Kursel waved his cap and declared "I shall stay with the ship." He and another sailor kept one gun firing until Japanese **torpedoes** struck. Von Kursel and many of his shipmates went down with the *Suvorov*.

The Russian fleet lost eight battleships and most of its smaller ships. Four thousand Russian sailors were killed. Japan won a famous and important victory.

▼ The Japanese battleship *Mikasa*, which was used in the battle of Tsushima, has today been repaired and preserved.

During World War I, there was only one big battle between **battleships**. In 1916, British and German **fleets** clashed at Jutland in the North Sea. After Jutland, new warships decided battles: **submarines** and **aircraft carriers**.

Who attacked Pearl Harbor?

The aircraft carrier first showed its might in World War II. This war started in Europe in 1939, but until 1941 the United States was still at peace. Then, on 7 December 1941, Japan attacked Pearl Harbor, a US naval base in Hawaii. Japanese carrier-planes hit eight US battleships with bombs and **torpedoes**.

▼ Here you can see US sailors watching as the Japanese attack ships at Pearl Harbor.

A lucky escape

George D. Phraner was a sailor on the *Arizona*. He had just eaten breakfast when he heard planes and saw smoke. As the planes flashed overhead, he saw they were Japanese. He ran to his gun.

The gun had no shells, so George and some other men rushed down five decks for more. That saved his life. When *Arizona* was hit, he was below the explosion. One thousand, one hundred and two of *Arizona*'s sailors died.

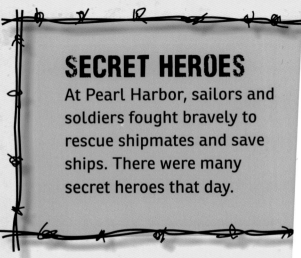

SECRET HEROES

At Pearl Harbor, sailors and soldiers fought bravely to rescue shipmates and save ships. There were many secret heroes that day.

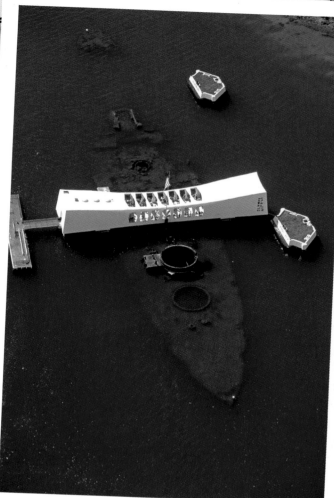

▶ This memorial to *Arizona* at Pearl Harbor is built over the sunken remains of the ship.

San Francisco's war

The United States **cruiser** *San Francisco* was docked in Pearl Harbor for repairs in 1941. It escaped the Japanese attack and was soon back at sea.

Cruisers against battleships

On 12 and 13 November 1942, *San Francisco* and other US ships fought Japanese battleships near the Pacific island of Guadalcanal. Fighting started at night. Searchlights and guns flashed in the darkness. The Japanese ships battered the cruiser *Atlanta* and then turned their guns on *San Francisco*. Admiral James Callaghan was killed, so his crewmate Bruce McCandless took command, even though he had been wounded.

NUMBER CRUNCHING

San Francisco was a fast cruiser, with a top speed of 32 **knots**, or 59 kilometres (37 miles) per hour. Launched in 1933, the ship fought throughout World War II. It was scrapped in 1956.

How the crew saved their ship

San Francisco was riddled with shell holes. As water flooded in, Herbert E. Schonland and others battled to keep the ship afloat. Up on deck, Reinhard Keppler was fighting a fire. It had started when a Japanese plane crashed on to the ship. Keppler bravely dragged his shipmates to safety. Badly hurt, he kept his firehose working until he died. *San Francisco* was saved.

REMEMBERING BRAVERY

Bruce McCandless, Herbert E. Schonland, and Reinhard Keppler were each awarded a Medal of Honor for their bravery.

▼ After the battle with Japanese battleships, a navy officer enters *San Francisco* to inspect the huge hole in its side.

WARSHIPS UNDER FIRE

Imagine being in a metal tube 76 metres (250 feet) beneath the waves. You are one of 40 sailors inside a World War II **submarine** called *U-47*, also known as a U-boat.

It is hot and stuffy. The air stinks of engine oil and unwashed bodies. You are on a top-secret mission into enemy territory. The risk is great but you must be brave.

How did a U-boat sneak into a harbour?

Günther Prien was captain of *U-47*. In October 1939, it made a daring attack on the British navy at its base, Scapa Flow, in the north of Scotland. *U-47* slipped into the bay underwater. Prien later wrote, "It seemed as if the whole boat was holding its breath." The crew spoke in whispers.

Prien looked through his **periscope**. He could see one British **battleship**, HMS *Royal Oak*. Still hidden, *U-47* fired torpedoes, and *Royal Oak* sank in just 20 minutes. The U-boat slipped out to sea as the British hunted in vain for the unseen attacker.

REMEMBERING BRAVERY

U-47's crew got a heroes' welcome in Germany. But in March 1941, it was itself sunk and Prien went down with it. *Royal Oak* lies beneath the waters of Scapa Flow. It is now a protected **war grave** in memory of those who died.

▲ These U-boat sailors are sharing
a meal in their submarine.

Wolf packs

In World War II, **Allied** cargo ships carrying war supplies from the
United States to Britain steamed together in **convoys**. Crossing the
Atlantic Ocean was dangerous, because "wolf packs" of German
U-boats lay in wait. Many ships were sunk by the submarines, and
more than 75,000 seamen died between 1939–1945. About 18,000
U-boat sailors died.

USS *Cole*

On 12 October 2000, the US Navy **destroyer** *Cole* was in the port of Aden, in Yemen. It had stopped for fuel oil. Yemen was not a peaceful country, but Commander Kirk Lippold did not expect trouble. As the crew lined up for a meal, lookouts spotted a small boat heading their way. It was travelling at a dangerously high speed.

Open fire? Or not?

Cole had plenty of guns, but was not ready for battle. Petty Officer John Washak saw the boat, but Navy orders were: "Don't fire unless someone shoots at you." But then, suddenly, the boat crashed into the ship – and blew up.

Suicide attack

Terrorists had carried out a suicide attack. Their boat-bomb had blown a 13-metre (40-foot) hole in *Cole*. Seventeen American sailors were killed and thirty-nine were injured. The terrorists, who also died, were supporters of **al-Qaeda**.

Other ships brought medical aid. *Cole* was lifted on to a giant Norwegian rescue ship, and taken to the United States for repair.

A year later, the same group who planned the attack on the warship carried out the terrorist attacks in New York and Washington, DC on 11 September 2001.

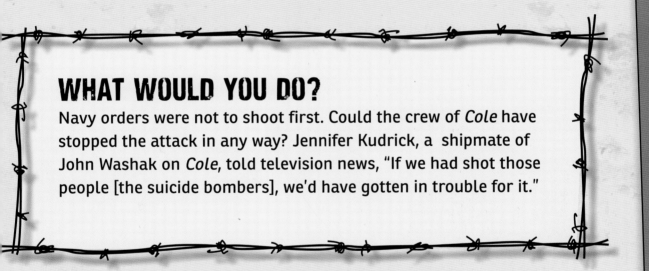

WHAT WOULD YOU DO?

Navy orders were not to shoot first. Could the crew of *Cole* have stopped the attack in any way? Jennifer Kudrick, a shipmate of John Washak on *Cole*, told television news, "If we had shot those people [the suicide bombers], we'd have gotten in trouble for it."

◄ This photograph shows the hole blown in *Cole*'s hull.

CONCLUSION

The attack on *Cole* showed that sailors face a new danger from terrorism. War at sea changes, just as ships do. Warships now have radar and computers to spot trouble, and missiles and guns to deal with it. But it is still the sailors who make the decisions.

Fighting pirates

Modern sailors combat one of the oldest dangers at sea: pirates! Pirates off the coast of Somalia in east Africa seize ships then demand money to set the ships and sailors free.

▲ Warships of many nations patrol the seas to protect ships from pirates and terrorists. Here, a Portugese team have captured some suspected pirates.

In April 2009, Somali pirates seized the US ship *Maersk Alabama*. The pirates sped out from the shore in motor boats and took Captain Richard Phillips captive. The ship's crew then drove off the pirates, but Phillips was still held in a lifeboat. Commander Frank Castellano in the **destroyer** *Bainbridge* tried to arrange a hand-over, but there were fears the pirates might harm Phillips or take him to Somalia. Sharp-shooters on *Bainbridge* took aim and shot three pirates dead. Captain Phillips was safe to return home.

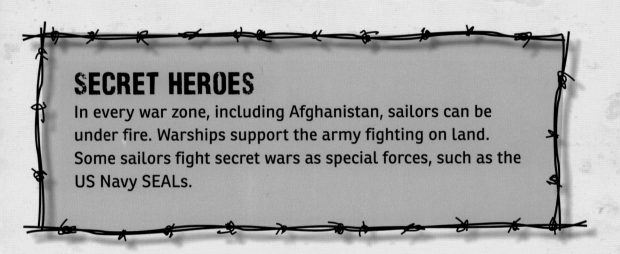

SECRET HEROES

In every war zone, including Afghanistan, sailors can be under fire. Warships support the army fighting on land. Some sailors fight secret wars as special forces, such as the US Navy SEALs.

Keeping the peace

Sailors today do not fight big sea battles. They help in land wars such as those in Iraq and Afghanistan. They fight terrorists and pirates. They protect trade routes on the oceans. They help people hit by floods, earthquakes, and other disasters. We still need sailors as much as we ever did.

SAILORS UNDER FIRE AROUND THE WORLD

USA
The surprise attack on Pearl Harbor by Japanese aircraft brought the United States into World War II.

USA
Mobile Bay was a battle during the American **Civil War**. It was one of the first battles between ironclad ships.

USA
John Paul Jones helped fight the British during the American Revolutionary War. He won respect for his daring and fighting spirit.

N
W ⊕ E
S

GREECE
At the battle of Salamis, the Persian **fleet** planned to smash the Greeks, but sailed into a trap. It was the Greeks who won this ancient battle between oared wooden ships.

RUSSIA AND JAPAN
Russia sent its battle fleet around the world to fight the Japanese. But the long voyage ended in a terrible defeat.

SCOTLAND
The attack by the *U-47* **submarine** during World War II showed that **battleships** were not safe even when they were in port.

YEMEN
The attack on *Cole* showed how much damage suicide attacks could do.

SPAIN
The Spanish **Armada** tried to land an army in England, to defeat Queen Elizabeth I. But the Spanish had underestimated the English navy, and the stormy seas around Britain.

ENGLAND
Trafalgar is the most famous naval battle in English history. Nelson's fleet won a famous victory in 1805, although he died at the moment of triumph.

PACIFIC OCEAN
The Pacific Ocean saw the biggest sea battles of World War II. Here sailors on ships like the **cruiser** *San Francisco* fought and died bravely.

GLOSSARY

aircraft carrier large warship from which planes can take off and land

al-Qaeda terrorist group founded in the late 1980s by Osama bin Laden

Allied nations fighting together during World War II, including the United States and the United Kingdom

Armada Spanish name for a large fleet of warships

battleship warship with large guns

cannon large, heavy type of gun that fires cannonballs

civil war war between different groups of people within the same country

Confederate one of the southern states in the United States that wanted to break away and form their own government in the 1800s

convoy group of ships sailing together, often for protection

cruiser medium-sized warship, common in the 20th century

destroyer small to medium-sized warship of today, armed with missiles

flagship ship on which the commander of a fleet travels

fleet group of ships sailing together

gunpowder explosive mixture of chemicals used in guns and rockets

knots unit of speed used to measure how fast boats travel. One knot is equal to one nautical mile per hour (exactly 1.852 kilometres per hour).

mine exploding weapon which can be hidden underwater

periscope submarine's viewing device that sticks up above the water

ram sharp, hard pointed front of a ship, for smashing holes in enemy ships

submarine ship that can travel under water

torpedo bomb that moves quickly under water and explodes when it hits its target

trireme Greek ship with three rows of oars on each side

Union states that made up the United States after some southern states tried to set up their own government in the 1800s

war grave last resting place of people who are killed in battle and have not been taken home

FIND OUT MORE

Books

Non-fiction

Tales of Invention: The Submarine, Louise Spilsbury and Richard Spilsbury (Raintree, 2010)

The Who's Who of: World War II, Clive Gifford (Wayland, 2009)

True Stories of the Second World War, Paul Dowswell (Usborne, 2007)

Fiction

Powder Monkey: Adventures of a Young Sailor, Paul Dowswell (Bloomsbury, 2006)

Websites

www.spartacus.schoolnet.co.uk/PRsearch.htm
Find out all about World War I and World War II on this website.

www.hmsroyaloak.co.uk
This website is dedicated to *Royal Oak*, the Royal Navy battleship sunk by *U-47* in 1939.

www.navy.mil
Have a look at the official US Navy website to learn more about what sailors do today.

A place to visit

The Imperial War Museum
Lambeth Road
London
SE1 6HZ
www.iwm.org.uk

Visit the Imperial War Museum to learn more about the wars discussed in this book.

INDEX